Film History

Film History

Poems by Al Maginnes

WordTech Editions

© 2005 by Al Maginnes

Published by WordTech Editions
P.O. Box 541106
Cincinnati, OH 45254-1106

Typeset in American Garamond by WordTech Communications LLC,
Cincinnati, OH

ISBN: 1932339930
LCCN: 2004117581

Poetry Editor: Kevin Walzer
Business Editor: Lori Jareo

Visit us on the web at www.wordtechweb.com

Thanks to the editors of the journals where these poems appeared:

32 Poems: "Chet Baker"
Asheville Poetry Review: "The Lion In the Backyard"
Atlanta Review: "Boys"
Brilliant Corners: "Ballads," "Where Late the Sweet Birds"
Controlled Burn: "Bluebird, Sparrow, What Lives Come To"
Crab Orchard Review: "The Endurance of Gospel"
Georgia Review: "For A Glass of Red Wine"
Greensboro Review: "A Movie Without an Ending"
Lake Effect: "The Vermeer Moment"
Laurel Review: "Stars Over Bedlam," "Toast," "The Song In the Background"
Louisiana Literature: "Translating the Dogwood"
Louisville Review: "Dark Shadows"
Melic Review (melicreview.com): "What Goes Unsaid"
Moonwort Review (moonwortreview.com): "The Language God Listens To"
Natural Bridge: "Townes Van Zandt 1944-1997"
News & Observer (Raleigh, NC): "Improvisation"
Nightsun: "The Burning Between Fires"
Pedestal (thepedestalmagazine.com): "Late Words for the Moon," "Outlasting Elegy"
Pleaides: "Thirst"
Poetry: "Before Electricity," "The Dignity of Ushers"
Poetry East: "Hour of Possibility," "Toolshed"
Quarterly West: "Honeysuckle and Menace"
Tar River Poetry: "Film History," "The Final Part of Dreaming," "Spirits," "Pornography"
Texas Review: "The Varieties of Silence"

Thanks to the North Carolina Arts Council for a fellowship that provided the time to write some of these poems.

For friendship, encouragement and specific advice on some of these poems, thanks to Betty Adcock, Joseph Bathanti, Mike Chitwood, Jim Clark (the younger), Suzanne Cleary-Langley, Susan Ludvigson, Rick Madigan, Kevin Prufer, Ron Rash, Kristin Scott, David Simonton, and Phil Terman. Thanks to Kevin Walzer and Lori Jareo at WordTech

Communications. And thanks to the faculty, staff and students of Wake Technical Community College.

This is in memory of James Whitehead, who taught me I would have to work to sing

And for Jamie, first and last

Contents

Before Electricity 11
Honeysuckle and Menace 13
Dark Shadows 15
The Lion in the Backyard 17
Boys 19
Guessing Distance 21
Film History 23
Improvisation 26
Chet Baker 27
Bluebird, Sparrow, What Lives Come To 29
The Varieties of Silence 31
The Space Men Claim 34
What Goes Unsaid 37
Drinking with Jim Thorpe 39
For A Glass of Red Wine 41
A Movie Without an Ending 44
Pornography 46
The Dignity of Ushers 48
Stars Over Bedlam 49
Late Words for the Moon 51
The Language God Listens To 52
Our Lives Happen In Rooms 54
Experience 58
Spirits 60
Thirst 61
The Needle's Task 63
The Blues and the Abstract Truth 65
The Endurance of Gospel 67
Outlasting Elegy 69
Townes Van Zandt (1944-1997) 70
"Where Late the Sweet Birds" 72
Ballads 75
Toolshed 77
The Abandoned Farm 78
The Vermeer Moment 81
Narrative and Dirge 83
The Final Part of Dreaming 87
Toast 89

Testimony 90
Translating the Dogwood... 92
The Burning Between Fires 93
The Song In the Background... 95
Hour of Possibility.. 97

Before Electricity

Evenings then were music, saw-grass rasp
of fiddle, thumb and horn-tipped fingers

frailing a reedy banjo, or the spinning forth
of words unspooled like thread to repair

the simple fabric lives were clothed by.
But once the lightning-born genie

of Franklin's kite came bottled and lay coiled
within walls like a snake, the world grew past

one row of trees picket-lining a field's edge
or the distant purple crown of a hill.

Conversations bustled past the death-bloated deer
on the road's margin, glimmer of new perch or bass

in root-lined ponds, to strike mothy flight
for distant and mostly invisible arenas of light.

Few mentioned how this hard new vision carved
faces and bodies, but more than one might have yearned

for the forgiveness smeary oil-light granted,
a glow built as much from shadow as from illumination,

when a wife shed the day's tired dress and reached
to let stiff hair fall. And before the room was

given wholly to dark, her husband might see
the mute instrument leaned in the corner,

its rust-scaled strings as silent as the two of them
lying in darkness that could dissolve too easily

to be trusted with any sound they might make.

Honeysuckle and Menace

Nothing in our lives is innocent.
Even slim tendrils of honeysuckle live
rooted in dark that warns hands away.
Bending to smell a flower might be
worth a snakebite on your mouth.
Down the street, a man slams his car door
over and over, yells for someone
to come outside and talk to him.
The shadows make homes for restless myth:
the boy who rose from the pond cloaked
in water moccasins, the leperous
old woman rumored to have poisoned
three husbands, Mister Gilmore who knows
hex-words to take away warts, uncoil
fire from burns. Believing everything
is our only choice. The note
sleeping in the long throat of summer
is not joy but the choking to speak
what we haven't learned to say.
Our bodies, the only things
this season trusts, demand exhaustion.
I threw the rock to feel my arm
whip forward, to snap
when motion stopped, not for the shock
of stone against flat glass
or how the window hung for one
vowel-long contraction before dropping
to splintered teeth. That morning,
I pulled at the tiny mouths
of honeysuckle, each offering
a tear on the unkissed tongue.
I will have to keep myself
from turning this to gold. One morning
the man who slammed his car door
will be put, handcuffed and weeping,

into a police car. We won't know why
so every word we hear will be gospel.
We pay for every sweetness we taste.

Dark Shadows

There were two directions home once the bell rasped
the school day shut, one more episode wound into the endless
reel of episodes. The first route yawned the length of Main Street, where
    only leaves moved
between pollen-stained houses. The quicker way went by Charles's Grocery
and the park scraped from dirt and sourgrass at the cusp of The Hollow,
that fist of streets that closed each afternoon around the invisible lives of
    our black classmates.

Because the dark veins of streets forms the borders that divide towns, we
    divided,
color from color, particle from particle, as we claimed different directions.
The habit and caution of hushed warnings kept any wary child from walking into
the narrow warren of streets where Mark Gamble, Regina Mabry, Deborah Bell
    disappeared
in the afternoons, the plaids and stripes of their school clothes lost among leaning
    porches, laundry hung
on worn cotton rope, cars and toys crippled and glazed by dust.

Black or white, we went home to watch *Dark Shadows*, whose title let us
    shiver in mock fright
over stories of vampires and time-frayed curses that never ended,
only spun into the next improbability, the bobbing of a theremin intended
to stitch together the scenes of mismatched narrative.
The next day our stories would be of the terror we felt,
this recited terror practice for the terror that waited, unrehearsed,

in empty lots, in the grid of burn marks on Cathy Sales's arm,
in the hands triggered to slap, in the questions with no answers sneering
out of the dark. There was Junior Dufray and his sleepy-eyed bunch
from The Hollow who smelled of cigarettes, old sweat, of bay rum gone stale,
who stepped in front of me some afternoon and patted my flat pockets,
the reek of their suggested violence a cold whisper, an echo, of the swollen lip

on the boy who wanted someone to fight him every afternoon, the sudden bloom

        of an eye swollen purple
and shut on the face of the girl who never spoke to anyone.
If fear is a story with no visible end but the twice-imagined specters that will
        leave us
and so do not end, then better the horror that can be switched off
when we begin to anticipate its repetitions. Better the overacted fear that grew
from the watery ghosts, the canned wolf-howls I finally stopped watching

as if all that frightened me could be ended so easily.
One story is what we leave behind, our bodies bearing us beyond
all our constructed alliances. The other story is what we fear
and how ruthlessly we deliver ourselves to the part of it we are able
        to name
while the other, sweeter part prowls unseen,
denying any name we could give it, denying it could be ours.

The Lion in the Backyard

When dusk gentles sky to charcoal-gray, when the quiet streetlights,
      the tawny window-lights wink on, only orbiting moths
and the house cats that quietly prowl night's depths still hear
      the harping of wild blood. But let the sky fall
to just the right shade, and I can hear again

the throaty call rising over roof-crests, over
      the churning of crickets and traffic hum
to tear a hole in the fragile curtain of our domesticity.
      No one could say what human impulse
delivered a lion to live out its days in a pen

in a North Carolina backyard, flanked by backyard grills and swing sets,
      matted with dust, ignored by all but the curious and the frightened.
The Wing brothers lived two blocks away, their front yard
      our summer night gathering place since
their mother would not complain, no matter how late or loud

we played the music or how often we walked
      behind the house to get high. One night
a minister, breath stained with non-sacramental wine,
      tried to recruit us to paint his church,
attempting to tame us with labor and shame, just as the lion's owner

might have dreamed of that beast dozing at his feet
      while he watched television or read scripture.
None of us laid a stroke of paint to a single holy board.
      In the long exhale of that summer's end, I led a girl
who refused to believe the lion's presence up to see for herself.

Its tail switched as we approached, its chesty growl
      bloody promise that it hungered to escape,
to stalk the savannas of our suburbs, the shorn grass
      of lawns poor camouflage for its lurking
in the subtractions of light between houses, its prey

not careless zebras or gazelles but mailmen, meter readers,
        the weak, clumsy walkers hidden behind flimsy doors.
We watched the malevolent yellow eyes watching us,
        the air we breathed, the dirt we stood on, transformed
by that regard. The quickening of her breath,

her nipples, small roses of flesh, dimpling the thin fabric
        of her shirt, testified to how the body fevers
when mortality is teased by a greater appetite.
        In the eyeblink of our turning away, metal chimed
as the lion hit the chain link barricade, pushing

into the thin wire holding him from the free-roaming world,
        shaking the plywood ceiling of the pen, boards
that might have built his only view of heaven.
        Alarm thinned our blood; I steered her away,
not down the trail of streetlights to the Wings' house

but up a nearly hidden path that neighbored a brown pond.
        We curved together while full dark covered us
like a drop cloth. And through the rattle of high grass,
        the tearing of our own open-mouthed breath,
the long vowels of the lion's voice magnified our shaking.

Boys

What invisible wires twitch the grimed hands
        of the unlovely teenage boy sipping coffee
the waitress made him pay for before
        she would serve him? The regulars' voices ground
to a slow halt when he sat at the counter, smell
        of leaf-mold and weather trailing him.
And some eyes still measure him while the dissection
        of morning news resumes.

Today the news is filled with a boy who killed
        his parents and two classmates, shooting
until his gun was emptied. In the last months,
        a handful of boys, drunk on rage and firepower,
have murdered, tiny snakes turned quickly,
        suddenly deadly. Those well-scrubbed faces
from the front page share nothing with this boy,
        his veil of dirty hair and nose stud,

his nails rimmed with chipped polish.
        Whatever rage he owns was ground
to powder long ago, dissolved in the rain he slept in
        last night, scattered across the map
of recent history. The coffee drinkers blame the President,
        suggest arming teachers, move on to sports.
Fat thumbprints of rain blot the windows,
        darken the sidewalk, as if the sky,

bloated after a big meal, loosened its belt
        and sighed, sealing us in here,
leaving me to sip the same black liquid
        the boy is drinking and ponder
the bottomless cup of rage
        those gun-toting boys drank from,
where I wet my beak more than once
        when my body was all projectile,

the world a target I couldn't hit,
> no matter how loudly I exploded.
I had to walk a lot of nights through rain
> before I understood how small
my anger was, how it would always join
> the world's collection of angers
and wash away, like the drops that make
> this unbroken rain, each one aimed at something.

Guessing Distance

If we speak of the dazzle and spin
delivering first proof of what lies
beyond any boy's half-grown ken,
we have to admit the reluctance
of any machine to commence labor,
the chain an arthritic creak, gears
staggering with human freight.
Riders, raised above bleached dirt
and tangle of river-limbs, love
leaving names and tired skin
but love even more dropping back
whole into all they have been.
But this boy is ravenous to become
a story of distance, blue smoke
crossing a range of roof peaks,
one flash in the fire-wreath
night wears. Earlier tonight,
he threw away money
on the duck shoot, the bottle toss,
the booth where age and weight get guessed.
Now cotton candy and fried dough,
even the snake-thighed dancers
in the tent he's too young to enter,
do not hunger him so much
as the black, starless miles
hidden beyond burning lights.
In the heart-blink that holds
rising from falling, when
the body seems poised to vanish
into fire, he knows
this field will soon stand empty,
but his lot has been cast
with the neon bloom of night's
roulette wheel and the migrant dust
that burns hot as stars in his chest

until even gravity turns uncertain
though trembling legs root him
to the ceaseless fire that feeds
the cold vacuum of dirt-life.

Film History

So I find you again, Dr. Stevens,
not in a classroom's closed universe
but in the tinhorn piano that scored
the silent movie I half-watched last night,
echo of you providing "Blood and Sand"

or "The Gold Rush" with a live soundtrack
on the classroom piano. I find you
tucked in the titles of films you mentioned
in class, saying one film leads to another
while their names filled my notebook's margins.

Entering your dusty basement domain,
the only classroom in the building with
a piano, we were barely aware
film could claim a history. Sitting among
desks and furniture stored and unwanted,

we watched the same ninety seconds
of film run until we breathed every nuance
of its making. When you stepped in the cone
of grainy light the projector scooped
from the room's semi-dark and pointed to

some unfelt presence we had missed, the scene
kept unreeling in the wrinkles and folds
of your shirt. Too much of what you said has gone
like the commands cornermen bark at fighters
between rounds or the instructions teachers call

into the push of students leaving class,
but the scene from the film always spooled forth
the same way, and the day your body became
your enemy, showed us the depths of
our inadequacy has not changed either.

The bow-tied grad student still threads the film.
The two girls in front of me ask each other
what you have just said. The fitful lights buzz
and dim as they have since our first day of class.
And you fall from the middle of your sentence

to the floor and land with a sound I heard once
when a side of beef smacked a concrete slab.
We see what has happened. None of us moves.
Does the air grow too thick for us to breathe?
Like a fighter hearing eight, you stand

in the newly-charged room. No one sees the screen
your hand waves at. This is drama beyond
the refinements of plot. Here is conflict:
the boxer ordered to dive, the drifter
enticed into murder by the boss's wife.

You fall again. This time we help you up,
fetch water, loosen your tie. Medics, grim
as townspeople in a black and white Western
who watch the outlaws arrive, wheel you out
of the room. With a tongue that has forsaken

language, still you want to speak. You will return
to finish the term, but never again
will the air spark as it did in those moments
of our helplessness. Never again will
movies—now they are only movies again—

be more than shadows pretending life
and their stories—students who inspire
a professor bitter with hard failure,
the delinquents redeemed by knowledge—
will only be ciphers, figures eclipsed

by the vision we saved of one who felt
the universe tilt but who rose before
our screen-blank faces to fall again,
alone with his single instinct to stand,
to stand and tell us what we did not know.

Improvisation

The legend says the lighthouse keeper
brought his young bride to the island
where they would live alone. To break
her isolation, he bought a piano.
Only one piece of music came
with the piano, and she played
this tune, matching its cadences
with the ceaseless ocean, endlessly,
until it became a hellish drum
fevering both their brains.
Mainlanders told of hearing the troubled notes
scrolling across the water, of the wife hiding
when visitors came, only to begin,
halfway through the visit, playing
that unnamed song again, her tone and speed
the same each time, her music unmarked
by any skill for improvisation. And, unerringly,
her husband swallowed the prescription
for madness, taking an ax
to the instrument's unsmiling teeth.
When the lighthouse was mute that night,
mainlanders came to the island
and found them both dead, the piano
that delivered the unvarying song
of their final days destroyed.
The music that haunts me most
is built on improvisation, written melody
a door for the music to exit through,
a way to let the story find
a less predictable ending.
On the CD recording of "Thelonius Himself,"
we can hear twenty minutes of Monk
trying notes, haggling with Orrin Keepnews,
as he teaches himself "Round Midnight," this tune
he will never play the same way twice.

Chet Baker

The late recordings, the voice
scorched to a fragment, mouth sore
with playing against the shift
of false teeth, are the ones
I come back to, like a man
who searches his pockets
for what he knows is not there.
New language makes the tongue
careful, concerned that a request
for coffee could harbor
lethal insult. Something slow
in Chet Baker's horn always sounded
as if he was just learning
the secret language of the tune,
discarding what didn't matter.
And what finally mattered
was the drug that outlasted
all the bandmates in quartets,
quintets, pick-up sessions,
outlasted the glorious
afternoon he made Bird's band
without an audition, outlasted
the looks that could have offered
the movie career America insists on
for her successful children,
outlasted all but the desire
that honed his body
to a melody of pure longing.
Such longing let his voice
discover the ache buried
in some impossibly sugared lyric
and make it into music
that might outlive the mouth
filled with pain, the throat worn raw
with cigarettes and vodka,
with talking to the ones

who would not go home but stayed
until he lost the simplest words,
stayed until he stood to walk
once more down the long barrel
of night to a room he knew
from the moment he checked in
that he would have to leave
before he was ready.

Bluebird, Sparrow, What Lives Come To

What sacrificial impulse brought
a bluebird, rare as snow in these parts,
to land in front of my car
so quickly I identified it only as I swerved,
as it lifted into its own vanishing?
The birds we believe most beautiful
we see only in flashes. Their instinct
is what I admire, the willingness
to claim new directions with the first hint
of trouble. It's easy to believe they know more
than we do. Listen to the ragged chorus
they make on a warm morning. Surely
all that music is saying something.
So what if they have thumbnail-
sized brains, a gram for a heart?
They can do what we can't. I lived
a short while in a rooming house
filled with hollow-chested men
whose lives were defined by their inability
to leave. Checks in the mail brought
rent and wine. At night the house filled
with the grim rasps of their breathing,
the noise of low-flying lives
resisting the impulse to land. Because they knew
I would not be staying, some told me
their stories. There was always
a woman, always a tragic miscarriage
of fate. More than once I praised
a figure barely more than silhouette
in a sepia-tinted portrait, keepsake
of some long-ago county fair or shore leave,
nearly erased by years of fond scrutiny.
Now beauty was luxury they could no longer afford.
Dusk discovered them perched along
the front porch, smoking unfiltered cigarettes

with the peculiar peace of beings
whose dreams and abilities have finally met.
Any restlessness resolved itself
with the touching of old scars, tracing
the blurred outlines of a tattoo.
If they noticed the sparrows scrabbling
through dust before thrumming into flight,
they never said a word.

The Varieties of Silence

1.

The curve of the phone receiver pressing my ear was
        the same hard plastic as the small shovel I used
to turn over sand during sun-blurred afternoons
        on the beach when my mother smoothed suntan oil
into her legs and leaned back, her eyes never so closed
        she couldn't keep track of my sister and me.
On one of those gravel-strewn beaches I first held
        a shell to my ear, trying to take the ocean's
message. And the ear not buried
        in the shell heard the progress of waves;
the other heard only the swelling of air
        that made all sound distant as the dusty tones
that overlap and hollow deep in the thought-quick
        thickets of fiber optics, that grow deeper while I wait
for a phone three hundred miles away to ring.

2.

When The Grateful Dead were recording *Aoxamoxoa*,
        a record as pieced together as a collage,
Bob Weir told the engineer that for one track
        he wanted the sound of "thick air." "Thick air,"
yelled the engineer just before leaving for good. "He wants
        thick air." The long vistas without sound
that some experimental compositions call for
        ask the listener to learn variations
in air's hovering frequencies. When we can listen
        to such stillness, the composer might claim,
then we are ready to hear music.

3.

For two days we barely speak, presences
        grim with politeness, our suddenly strained orbits
veering just close enough that we are
        excruciatingly able to place the other at all times.
In such avoidances we risk kinship with
        the leftover malevolences we call ghosts,
our unexpelled breath chaining our lives
        to our meaty sighs and clamorous steps.
At different times we've both lived
        in houses proclaimed haunted by local superstition,
and that could excuse the unexplained
        sigh of wood or closing of a door
no one passed through. But this stiff quiet
        that demands permission or apology
for each sound makes us desire
        the banter that makes the usual furniture
of our rooms, itself another form of not speaking.

4.

What I loved about heroin was falling
        into silence that demanded no answer.
At such times it was easy to understand
        a life measured out
by weights and spoons. But it was silence too full
        to be listened to for long.
After being told I had hepatitis, I told no one
        for weeks, practicing a new brand of silence
because to break it was to say
        what I had no desire to name.

5.

Soon, a few minutes, an hour, I'll walk
        into the room where you are and break
our two-day silence. Some white noise and compression
        would have pulled the drone of thick air
from the studio speakers, the same hum or a cousin
        of the noise that curled deep within a seashell
and vanished when I moved it from my ear.
        If it were only the noise of a shell clamped
over an ear, the techniques of making thick air
        or the drowsing valley of opiates, silence
would matter no more than most sound. But those variations
        are leaky craft, fit only to bring us
closer to the island we launched from, closer to
        the birth-broken silence that forms one parentheses
of the open-ended silence our life is.

The Space Men Claim

The three women on the couch swayed like music, glasses
                of wine tilting,
their shoulders pressed tight, legs touching and moving away

                as they improvised a comfort
men will not permit themselves in such close arrangements.
                For three hours, I sat shoulder

beside shoulder with the husband of one of these women and another man
                in a minor league ballpark,
our nearness only allowed by the armrests that defined each man's territory,

                space so uncertain
another friend and I used to leave a seat between us in the movies.
                Coming back from the game,

we were talking Zen and I mentioned the lecture I'd read
                on creating "Buddha-space"
as the lecturer called it. There was no space for Buddha

                on that couch unless
he was the size of the angels said to dance by the billions
                on the heads of pins,

but angels are mostly wishful air, their bodies negligible and able
                to pass through one another,
unlike our arrangements of solid mass around a core

                of dark light, of air that uses
all it touches and leaves nothing, only bodies that dream
                they are capable

of doing what they cannot. When quiet crossed the just-turned fields
                around the house where I lived
one nearly-forgotten spring, I would be on my feet

     and leaving before I knew
where exactly I was going. But one night rain came in fitful spits
      and my cold thumb had

little hope of stopping any cars. So when watery brake lights flashed
      and a car fish-tailed
to a stop, I wondered if I wanted this ride. But I had hitched

     enough rides to handle
whatever came my way. The car accelerated before
      my door closed, tires loud

on the wet road. The driver was alone, faceless as I probably was
      in the dark, and when
he asked if I wanted a blow job, his big hand suddenly gripped

     my thigh, not like
a would-be lover but so hard that tendons ridged
      the back

of his spidery hand. Days later I would have fingerprint bruises
      on my leg. And for days,
the memory of that hand, half-visible in the glow of dash-light

     would burn through
each tiny wilderness the body shelters, distorting
      whatever time it took

to loosen that grip that has never quite let go.
      The first night I slept
with her, a tornado rocked our town and I gripped her

     even in sleep, fearing perhaps
that if I weakened my hold, our bodies might no longer curl into
      this easy accommodation.

My father refused all accommodation, worked and smoked till he outran
        his body. Once he and I dug
holes to plant fast-growing photinas, a fence line along

        the single square of earth
he called his own. Like him, I believe in the body's weight,
        not the empty chambers

beyond our touch. But the three women on the couch moved
        as if body might pass
through body and hold its shape, as if the barriers men learn early

        to raise might be dissolved
and reformed, illusion those women could luxuriate in
        because they knew

the body's real boundaries, not the ones negotiated
        by the fear that leads men
to build fences, clutch their partners in sleep, to create the spaces

        we will not let our bodies fill.

What Goes Unsaid

Because quiet equaled strength in the movies
you grew up on, because your father's example
was silence, you find yourself maker and giver
of laws, not the benign patriarch you dreamed yourself.
So when your daughter crosses an uncrossable line,
backing you into the corner where heroes are defined,

you play your last card and order her from your house,
sentencing yourself to nights of anxious regret
you'll spend driving the roads around the handful of places
she still mentioned to you, searching for her or one
of the pierced and strangely dressed friends who never spoke
when you were around. On the second night of this,

you think you see her under a streetlight, but she's gone
by the time you get there. First boy in your class
to pierce his ear, veteran of uncounted disputes
over clothes and hair, adept at prodding parents
from silent contemplation of a meal to careless rage,
how many nights did you slam the door behind you,

run into night's silence? How many times, hero
of your own unscripted movie, did you dodge
the sweeping gaze of your father's headlights? If you try,
you can still taste the dirt on the potatoes you dug
out of hard-frozen ground and had to chew down raw
when your final match could not get a fire started.

You would never be so grateful for your father's silence
as you were two nights later when he found you, drunk
on Irish Rose and throwing up between two cars.
And now you understand his silence was not strength
but fear. And it is fear you feel driving to the house
where one of her friends says she might be found, but you walk

through the door like John Wayne or Clint Eastwood coming
to have it out with a bunch of drunken rustlers.
There are no rustlers here, only two thin-armed boys
too wrecked to offer any menace, and your daughter,
gray-faced and limp as string, passed out on a couch.
Going home, she squirms and murmurs sounds you translate

into thanks, and you want to believe she will no longer
hide behind silence and you will be the parent
you wanted for yourself. But when she sits with you
a few nights later to watch one of those movies
that make justice a simple thing, neither of you speaks,
mute before a screen where speech is always a weakness.

Drinking with Jim Thorpe

When the burning silk of liquor jaded
his throat, time slipped unmoored from the hands of
David, my great-uncle, to reconstruct
Canton, Massillon, Dayton, those old scars,
knuckle-tough towns where he played football
for money, a new team each season,
his version of homesteading or prospecting,
some American quest that turns work to myth,
before football became a TV pageant
of bright uniforms and outsized platoons.
The famous names he played with and against

provided currency for the stories
he started and never finished, or this one
that he did not tell and would not have
even if it had been true: late Sunday,
sky going the angry blue of bruises
he feels but will not admit, David walks
past glass storefronts that make most of what he knows
of this town. Years from now, he'll see a picture
of this afternoon's game, men who seem formed
from mud as much as muscle rearing out of
spike-clawed earth to be knocked flat again.

He will not be able to find himself
in the mud-shrouded scrimmage but will point
accurately as a compass needle to
the man who looms around the corner now.
Jim Thorpe, big enough to block what little light
there is on this street, the way he blocked
two of Massillon's Tigers this afternoon,
setting David free for an eighty-yard run.
For a month they have played in the backfield
without speaking, even posing side-by-side
for the team picture without a word,

David waiting for Thorpe—a man already
famous for years, who has eaten with presidents,
been decorated by kings—to speak first.
And he does.
                    "Nice run today." They walk
the same direction, one of them turning
around to accommodate the other.
Thorpe's silence swallows David's questions
about baseball, the Olympics, the medals
Thorpe had to return but could not surrender.
Jim Thorpe pulls a bottle from his pocket,
takes a drink, then offers it to my uncle.

Our lives build themselves on the moments between
acceptance and refusal. Who could see,
in that silent offer, the half-gallons
of gin that would become the centerpiece of
my uncle's table, the wife—his fourth—who poured
his first one each morning, the one that stopped
his hands' shaking and let him dream backward
through vanished wives, failed businesses, the gains
fumbled away as he drank to his future
on a street corner in Ohio at dusk.

For A Glass of Red Wine

       I want to reach over and move you
so your smoky odor of crushed grape
       cannot drift around me, but
I cannot stop watching the smear
       of candlelight reflected on your ruby belly,
bright as the hourglass marking
       the black widow I killed in my tool shed
this summer. Once I loved
       your mystery uncoiling on my tongue,
the dark and gleaming veins you opened there.
       And I loved your earthy cousin, beer, the one
who bears the brassy accent of wheatfields,
       and your sullen friends bourbon, scotch and rum
who might end the party singing
       sad Irish songs or smashing furniture
and beating the host. But what
       I loved, finally, was the blackness you brought,
the stars dying one by one. I kissed you good-bye
       long ago. Still, when I see mouths purse
with meeting you, see the dim coal
       of an eye suddenly waken, I recall
your first kindliness, blood-glow
       I could believe for the length of your burning,
rapture I could ride until pre-dawn woke
       fear of what forgotten hours held.
But if I could believe your first singing moments
       once more, diamonds flaring against velvet
to deny the dust stones become,
       I'd grab you from where you sit
and swallow, pouring one emptiness
       into another until we are two
hollow bells ringing to be filled
       and filled again until the swirl commences
once more, swirl of voices and light,
       of blood, tiny cyclone

in the clear barrel of a syringe, swirl now
        of my wine-colored blood in tubes taken
to be tested and measured, to tell me
        how far this new disease has marched,
how far this medicine might push back
        the death I see resting there
as surely as I see it squatting
        in the black core of every bottle, every tilted
glass of wine. "Kill it," Keith Greenway urged,
        passing me the last bird-sip of bourbon
he'd hoarded by small doses from
        his father's bottles, the first time
I surrendered to the gentle rocking
        held there. I was fourteen.
"You could have been killed," I'd hear
        for the next seventeen years, after
the car wrecks, bar fights, nights in jail,
        nights passed out in corners
or empty lots, all the baggage
        a good drunk knows is part of the trip.
But now, I know that for many of those years
        of passing out and waking up, my death
dwelled inside me: the unknown years
        my liver smoldered, shriveling
around this disease I just learned the name of,
        that's led me to a regimen of pills
and injections more strict than any
        I've ever answered, even more strict
than the stone-thick craving for you
        I still carry. The slow burning
of my liver might stall or even reverse,
        but one scent of your dry breath
can make me thirst again
        for the cup after cup I emptied,
searching, I thought, for the pearls
        some kings used to hide in wine

for favorites of the court to find,
 round and drowning
and, briefly, the color of blood.

A Movie Without an Ending

Lost in memory's long fall into shadow,
the three movies that could be seen for sixty cents
as the Palace Theater spun its slow last waltz,
a costume jewel wobbling on the withered hand
of a fading downtown block, but all summer
while I changed buses, going to and from
my first job, those titles waved
from the unlit marquee, a beckoning
I finally obeyed long enough to slide a dime

and two quarters to the night-pale blonde woman
who didn't look up or move the smoldering
white peg of cigarette from her savagely lipsticked mouth,
but scraped my coins into the drawer
and pointed me in with a canine-sharp red nail.
Whatever figure once lived in the lobby's carpet,
mended now with long swaths of silver tape, had been walked
featureless by the million feet my feet followed
past the glass case of shriveled yellow popcorn,

the two fat hippie girls giggling behind the counter,
the wall mural of blocky figures, a WPA salute
to the green muscle of irrigation, its colors now bleeding
into the swirls of stuccoed wall. The yawning dark
yielded no color but the lit screen. The flickering
cathedral-sized room, the domed cupola of ceiling
bespoke a half-seen and fading elegance,
reminder of days when dreams came packaged
more elaborately, when men wore hats and women gloves

to visit the movies, and touched politely
when they danced. But when I sat, I sat deep
in the gravity of ruin, my feet rustling food wrappers
stuck to the floor. The sour fume of spilled beer
and cigarettes, of bodies stale with not moving,

said that this was the unlit side of the world
I was, at sixteen, growing into, working
forty-five hours a week in a warehouse, carrying,
I thought, weight the equal of any grown man.

When a man in front of me turned and handed back
the burning ember of a joint, I took it and smoked
while his head rolled to his chest and he spit forth
a chest-rattling snore. The screen became a collage
of gunshots, car crashes and close-ups of hard-faced men
and models whose capped teeth gleamed above bathing suits.
But the movies were decoration, backdrop.
The real drama sprawled around me, drinking wine
jacketed in paper bags, sleeping or bumming smokes.

This was distance greater than the two long bus rides
from my safe and quiet neighborhood. No artifice
of plot waited to save the bent and tired men
around me, the ones twitching in grim and dreamless sleep,
yet this shrine to fantasy held on, promised each one
darkness in which all things are possible,
where a woman, fresh with the scent
of lemons, might press her body against his
and sing the raptures of an invisible orchestra.

My eyes opened on a car blossoming into fire.
Somewhere behind me a bottle hit the floor,
whiskey-furred laughter cackled upward. I stood,
stumbled over a sleeper whose gloved hand
fisted an empty pint. The girls in the lobby stared
through the mural's unmoving screen. The sidewalk lay
empty and brooding, but with Hollywood's sure timing,
the bus arrived to ferry along night-jeweled streets, ushering
light across the empty screen I called my life then.

Pornography

How would I have come to it but through the damp pages
        of old *Playboy*s stashed in the woods behind Greg Dial's house,
tiny circles of mildew like decayed stars marking the bodies
        we gawked and gawked at? So maybe
the confusion started there, the wondering whether
        this was a sacred vessel we stared at or something to cast aside
once the need was done. My computer screen fills
        with offers for time shares, lower mortgage rates, invitations
to Brandi and Tiffany's web-cammed dorm room
        where all major credit cards are accepted, where
a glassed-in passion mocks the fever that opened
        those damp magazines, portals that offered the first
inkling of what might be though the pleasure they extended lay
        so distant no rank and futile dreaming could touch it.

But that is not what I'm talking about. Nor am I speaking
        of flesh suddenly real, of the first time my fingers brushed
through rough hair and curled to touch what folded
        underneath, those mute regions hidden so long
I could have doubted their existence, could have believed them
        one more horny legend, like mountain oysters or men
and boys who coupled with goats, if I had not seen
        the glossed and airbrushed pictures that proved
the truth behind rumors of that long-sought delta. So when
        Dallas Mangum gave his nuts a hoist and promised
to wear out some split-tail tonight, I believed, even though I knew
        he would end the night passed out in his car, sleeping
in the shadow of the closed-down pool hall. And I believed again
        when the first girl who let me in surged beneath me.

Pleasure so short-lived may deserve only the passive face,
        the stilled half-smile practiced by the motionless women
in photographs. Yet mine was the face clamped silent
        as her breathing and her voice dredged forth a language
buried in the oldest valleys and tides the body holds,

        something no snapshot coyness or cottony movie clip
made me ready for. Once I looked in the window
        of a novelty shop festooned with rubber and plastic devices
that make parody or ritual from our need for other bodies,
        that, like the techniques men's magazines offer
in clinical detail, reduce all passion to manipulation,
        a progression to a desired result. The masks
staring from the walls, black leather sacks designed
        to make us faceless, erased my gaze.

If we are anything more than vehicles for body parts
        dependent on friction, it comes from our ability
to construct the face behind the mask, the fluid wince
        and grimace the model's pose denies. These nights
I walk upstairs to sleep beside a woman who is
        my life's good fortune. And if, once or twice, I followed
the computer's pointed finger to Brandi and Tiffany's room,
        isn't curiosity the unextinguished part of desire?
Worse to me now are the times I rose and dressed
        for my own vanity, times I was steered not by affection
but by icy appetite and the need to add to some hidden tally
        that wanted nothing to do with the first open-eyed gazing,
the spear-thrust of a desire that believed in the beloved
        grace of every breathing body I would touch.

The Dignity of Ushers

Their authority did not unfold
from ironed white shirts and thin ties
or from the funereal seriousness that struck
their acne-splashed faces but because
they stood heir to our native faith in light.

So we followed the thin white waver
of beams they pointed down aisles
to seats we never thought of refusing.
It was the first job I wanted,
especially after birthday outings

far from home showed me the glowing
outfits worn by big-city ushers, their get-ups
a blend of doorman and military dictator,
as gaudy and fine as the plots
of movies my Saturdays were swallowed by.

None of us knew, as they took us
into the artificial light of the cinema,
that they walked the path of the pin setter,
the blacksmith or elevator operator,
professions reduced to curiosity

by wandering time. Only in the quick steps
of floor salesmen, the slim backs of hostesses
bringing us to our tables, do they remain,
the artful flutters of their flashlights lost
in dark we are left to find our own way through.

Stars Over Bedlam

Because the streetlight on the new road
behind our house outshines the country-mouse moon,
to see the stars we would have to walk
a long way across fields allotted to the state hospital
for the insane, until, out of sight
but not out of hearing of the road,
we could lie on our backs,
block our eyes against the white glow
that hangs over cities and be soaked
into the skewed geometries of sky.
But each star would echo the eyes I imagine
at every window of the hospital,
quiet and watchful as the moon,
dead and coveted stone
once believed to govern the mad's unruly tides.
In movies, the mad scream their torments,
but that hospital's green lawns and narrow lanes
have always been thick with the hush
that follows calamity, night's medicated silence.
Your madness could not be silent.
You sang operas composed that moment,
gave flowers to strangers, tipped a cab driver
seventy dollars for a seven-dollar ride.
One function of our double-sided hearts
is to know desire and its shadow,
to know such joy must pay a price.
Your blessing was believing it all came free.
Some tribes have made oracles of the mad,
have been steered by their moon-touched whims
the way some now follow the shifting sky,
travel for days to touch the altars
of pagan goddesses, as if answers live
only where most of us have never been.
When you came back to work, your music
muffled by Lithium, we watched you

as closely as any astronomer ever watched
the heavens, sure that some answer lived there
if only we had the language to ask.

Late Words for the Moon

There you are, old moon, old rock-in-the-sky,
still holding when I rise on shaky legs
for water to wash the bitter powder
of the sleeping pill from my tongue. How have I come
so untethered from your pull I must be chained
to the time-release anchor of these capsules?
Tonight, all I have failed to do seems important.
You, first marker of man's aspiration
to heaven, should understand that. Tonight,
the slow disease that percolates in my liver strips
too much of the world to the bones sleeping
beneath each silken veil. Centuries of poets
have sung to you, dressed you in the faces
of their beloveds. My house is dark, and you
and I are face to face, my blood becoming syrup,
the pitted lozenge of your face a chart
of where I have not been. Let me look at you
without forgetting how the pill dissolves in water.
Let me find the right notes to make hymns
to speculation and desire. I know men have mapped
your surface, given names to your valleys
and dusty ridges. I know the right machines would
let me stand on your surface like a street corner,
the way I'm standing here, one hand tight on this glass,
the other clutching the counter's edge. Let me be grateful
for the slow work of these pills. Let me come to you
another night with something like longing.
I know better than to believe you are listening.
But I have to say this, and there you are.

The Language God Listens To

I don't know what to say about the blackbirds
that angled over the bank parking lot this morning.
They were loud enough to make me look up,
as if sound is how they locate themselves in flight,
how they keep their destination before them
like tourists who, before the fatigue of long travel
descends, speak incessantly of where they're going.
For days, I've barely left my house,
caretaker to silence that arrives sometimes and stays
like a season that won't end, snow in April,
cold nights of spring sprawling into June.
We expect a lot. We want birds silent and beautiful.
We want to speak as if what we say means something
when the truth is we use language because
we've invented nothing better.
Tonight, there are letters being written to God
in every language, requests not his to grant or deny.
But he reads them all. The cup of dark wine
he drinks from is endless. He wishes for rain,
wishes heaven's busy-tongued birds could close
the cauldron of their infernal racket. He wishes
we had better handwriting. Sundays when I step outside
for the paper, the neighbors are leaving for church.
We wave. We don't speak much though we're friendly,
willing to lend mild labor or admire
one another's flowers, but we've never learned how
to weed out the awkward quiet that punctuates
        our small talk.
This morning I thought I heard gunfire and worried
that another neighbor—we all have one like this—
had lost it. Last month a man in Utah shot his daughter
because he heard the devil singing from her mouth.
An autopsy uncovered a grid of whip scars on her back.
They were so quiet, neighbors said. No one suspected a thing.
The sound I heard dropped into silence that is not silence

but small noise piled so deep around us we don't notice it,
wordless language I believe God prefers
because it asks for nothing, because he must tire
of talking only to the mad. God's life,
like the lives of the birds, has little to do with ours.
But he addicts us. And he must love
how we court him, struggling to bring him the right syllables
though our praise is the last offering he needs.

        beside the principal's office
where the worst offenders went. When that room grew noisy or full,
        Mr. Wilson, his hair

the iron-gray of tombstones, stooped blank-faced into the room
        and the flat smacking noise
his paddle made bounced down the throat-dark hall.

        But Jerry Luke returned
to a kind of solitary grace, no longer bothered
        for assignments not done,

no longer sent to the hall or called to play outfield,
        no longer, in fact, called
for anything, as our polite shunning became code, sharpened

        to draw blood
more quickly than a lifetime of blows and insults,
        each purgatoried hour

not erasing but darkening the front page photograph
        of Mr. Luke handcuffed
that was delivered to doorsteps all over town.

        At home, exile
to my room was intended as punishment
        and I would stare,

hot-eyed, at the patterns paint made on my door, each one
        singular as a fingerprint,
ignoring all the diversions hoarded behind me.

        And Jerry stayed silent,
the locked room we had assigned him barring entrance,
        until any attention

we might have awarded him became, like the room
        next to Mr. Wilson's office,
a place where greater punishment was possible.

        This story should have
some ending and I suppose it does, but Jerry didn't return
        to school after Easter,

so I don't know if he took up the quick and thoughtless violence
        that punished his father
or if, for him, we were stored in some empty room of memory

        just as he was for us.
Once as I arrived at a prison to teach a poetry workshop, I heard
        one guard say to another

"We got a special room for him," about some troublemaking inmate
        and I knew which room they meant.
Before entering the classroom, I wondered about finding

        faces I knew,
but none of the quiet men eyeing me recognized
        anything more than another

sweating functionary trying to sell the notion that
        his slim knowledge could
unlock doors. I didn't tell them that words or the unspoken

        promise of words pushed me
from the doors and fences, the special rooms,
        made to hold them.

Mantled in the same silence I had learned when the door
        to my room closed,
they sat convinced that words saved no one. But I began

      speaking the way I wish
Jerry had, speaking until we had no choice but to open
        the room we closed him in.

Experience

There's a point, still as the center
of a compass, when one believes
that most of what can happen has
already happened and all that comes
after this will be easy. The last time
I thought that, I was changing clothes
in a motel room. In an hour, I would
read my poems to an audience quiet
with wondering why they were wasting
a Saturday afternoon in April
listening to poetry. The mirror
on the closet door reflected the mirror
over the sink, and when I stood
between the two, I could see
the new thickness that swelled
my back and shoulders after
a year of afternoons in the gym,
hours I might have been writing poems
or reading Christopher Smart.
Not bad for forty one, I told myself,
buttoning the shirt I wore
to give readings that year.
Three weeks later the doctor called.
He told me *hepatitis*, a word
I'd always associated with *clematis*,
so I thought of gardens, of vines
and black flowers, of plants
whose predatory beauty, untended,
might smother all they touch,
the way morning glories once stampeded
the tomatoes in my father's garden,
wrapping them in a green web,
tiny purple flowers trumpeting sunrise,
singing my failure to do the weeding.
He said *hepatitis C*. I only knew

speaking the way I wish
Jerry had, speaking until we had no choice but to open
the room we closed him in.

Experience

There's a point, still as the center
of a compass, when one believes
that most of what can happen has
already happened and all that comes
after this will be easy. The last time
I thought that, I was changing clothes
in a motel room. In an hour, I would
read my poems to an audience quiet
with wondering why they were wasting
a Saturday afternoon in April
listening to poetry. The mirror
on the closet door reflected the mirror
over the sink, and when I stood
between the two, I could see
the new thickness that swelled
my back and shoulders after
a year of afternoons in the gym,
hours I might have been writing poems
or reading Christopher Smart.
Not bad for forty one, I told myself,
buttoning the shirt I wore
to give readings that year.
Three weeks later the doctor called.
He told me *hepatitis*, a word
I'd always associated with *clematis*,
so I thought of gardens, of vines
and black flowers, of plants
whose predatory beauty, untended,
might smother all they touch,
the way morning glories once stampeded
the tomatoes in my father's garden,
wrapping them in a green web,
tiny purple flowers trumpeting sunrise,
singing my failure to do the weeding.
He said *hepatitis C*. I only knew

of one kind, the kind that kept
Gary Carden out of school for six weeks,
the kind that turned old junkies piss-yellow.
The kind that went away.
One night, maybe the night
the tenacious virus entered my blood,
I stood before a terrarium
filled with carnivorous plants,
watched them stir and quiver
at heat and motion, swaying between
animal and vegetable. Bloodless,
they lived on blood, could have lived
on the blood running in the fat veins
praised by the first guy to hit me up,
his lanky fingers poking the inside
of my arm. Then we opened the soil
of my body and gave that vine
a place to take root. But before
the call from the doctor or remembering
the glass box of wet-looking plants,
I was just a man getting dressed
in a motel room, a man certain
that hard part was done. If I could
speak to him now, I would say
You think you're finished?
This has only started. Nothing
has happened to you yet.

Spirits

Though it's been over ten years
since I sipped any drink stronger
than coffee or non-alcoholic beer,
I still have a pulse of the old ecstasy
when I pass through the portals
of a bar. And while I believed neither
the turtle-backed Baptists of my youth
who called whiskey the devil's work
nor the inspired drunk who proclaimed
alcohol God's gift to man,
the mid-afternoon dim of a bar,
the slow upward winging of smoke
create a stirring in the soul, one reason
the ancients called them spirits.
It dreams for us. Lift a glass
and see what cloudy essence swirls there,
the unnamed name of what sings
deep within the choir of bottles.
And if the body cooks itself
above that blue flame, is twisted
in the shape of a tired bar rag,
we must know the pleasure continues
beyond pleasure. The first time
I went to the altar to let
wine become blood, I could not
suspect the opposite to be true,
that flesh could unravel
into alcohol, smoke, careless words
that drift ceaseless as prayer
from out bodies, vessels able
to be filled or emptied by spirits.

Thirst

From any distance, the corner restaurant's
burnished light and wide windows must make
a target, a harbor impossible to enter or ignore
for the city's night walkers who could once
claim that intersection as their own.
We were at the slow end of our meal, forks twirling
in the last strands of pasta, bread mopping
marinara sauce, when something struck
the front glass so hard it rattled,

so hard it stopped the hive-swarm of talk,
the chime of silver against china. My wife's story
broke in mid-stride as the six at our table turned
to see the man staring in, his furious gaze
swimming over us, palms pushed flat
against the pane as if he were straining
to execute a vertical push-up. He slapped the window
once more and staggered back, groping
for his drowned balance before sliding
out of our view, back into the nighthawk tide.

When her words stopped, Jamie was telling us
about water intoxicants, patients of hers
who swallow enough water to make themselves
drunk, the body's own wedding at Cana.
Someone wondered what kind of water
the man at the window was drinking,
but our nervous flutter of laughter was decoration,
unsatisfying as the ruffles of parsley on our plates.

And my mouth went hot with remembering
thirst I once thought would never quiet,
that screamed in my blood as I lurched down sidewalks,
as I dropped into slumber
too close to death. A little more time

and my body, desperate for submersion,
might have sinply become a wick
for that canned and bottled fire,
might have even learned to distill
water to its desperate pleasures.

The waiter, who had looked disgusted
when we did not order wine, hurried over
to tell us not to worry, the police had been called,
and to offer dessert or a glass of wine
on the house. I asked for more water.
One morning it was only my thirst and me.
I still could not say how I left it behind
or why it surfaces out of ash,
calling one of us to save the other.
There are mouths still clinging to the mouths
of glass bottles, pressing themselves to fountains,

burning and drowning at once
in thirst that is its own crucible.
In that rite, water becomes wine
which becomes the desire for wine
until water and wine are one body,
a sea to bless our drowning.

The Needle's Task

       After the first time, when the grinning man
who took hold of my arm and sang, "Here comes
           your nineteenth nervous breakdown," had eased

the mix of blood and drug into my vein,
           I waited in the place I wanted the dope
to hit, didn't consider the needle

           even years later when I had to shoot
medicine into the fat around my waist,
           trying to shake out the hepatitis

some night's long-forgotten injection had locked
           in one of my blood's shuttered rooms. I was
so far outside or inside myself, reading

           whether the cure worked or did not work,
the needle was again only the means
           of delivery, a pinch and then gone.

I've watched people mine bruised and broken-down arms
           for a vein, their entire bodies made
conduit for the drug, but when I swab

           my wife's hip before the shot of personal
or progesterone, I'm reminded that drugs
           sometimes stop working just when they are

needed, nature's odd design. Our friend has
           offered to make a gown for the child
we are trying to have. I've watched her sew,

           wondered at how her hands seem to let go
of the pain they are often fisted by
           when she fits shapes of cloth into a whole,

binds them with stitches quick and sure, needle
        bobbing like a bird that feeds on light
as she tugs the thread tight, hiding each hole

    a needle must make to do its work.

The Blues and the Abstract Truth

The Hawks visit Sonny Boy Willamson
Helena, Arkansas

Later they would tell of their shock
upon discovering he spit
in that can not tobacco juice
but blood. But they could say nothing
back to the deputy sheriff
who came to run them out of town
for eating in a black-owned joint
on the dirt-road side of Helena.

One short afternoon of playing
blues in a rented room, sipping
home-made liquor called Blind Tiger,
stood no chance of knocking over
measures more strict than the twelve bars
they'd swapped around all afternoon,
these five white boys called The Hawks
and one dying black man who still looked

sharp in his London-tailored suit,
strutting Helena's dusty streets.
Sonny Boy would soon be dead
and The Hawks would be on the road
with Bob Dylan, that afternoon
the slurred harp-notes history plays.
Then Dylan would fall from his bike
and they would become The Band.

That afternoon, Sonny told them
about his trip to London, about
the English boys whose names would soon

be on albums stashed in bedrooms
all over America: "They want
to play blues so bad, and they play
so bad." Last time I saw The Band,
Richard Manuel, soon to die, sang

"I Shall Be Released," his face burned
white in the spotlight, spectral,
as alone as Sonny Boy dead
in a borrowed bed, as alone
as the deputy who brought law
written nowhere but in the dust
on Helena's streets, in the blood
of men and women who walked there

through customs framed by decades
of power's silent arrangements.
This was what they had come to see,
what Sonny Boy couldn't tell them
when he spit blood in a coffee can,
then blew for all he was worth,
screaming out riffs time would let them
practice until they could play.

The Endurance of Gospel

The two microphones hovering over the musicians
        like the all-seeing eye of God
Sunday school teachers frightened us with
        missed nothing, not the twang of a wire string
stretched into harmony, the fiddle's back-sliding notes,

the whispered curse of the seventeen year old guitar player,
        Pigeon Creek still raw in his voice, already possessed
of lightning fingers and a fierce taste for whiskey, nervous
        about his first record but pleased
they would be singing songs his grandmother could listen to.

Because I was baptized in a church built of dark wood
        and stained glass and not dunked in a river
in full view of a congregation of cast-offs, cripples and mutes,
        the broken reeds of their voices swaying in the current
of a song of blood and redemption as I stepped back to land,

these hymns, recorded the year I was born,
        are as close as I can come
to the old churches tucked in the crooks of county roads,
        deserted except on Sundays
and sometimes even then. The songs make their own river,

where generations bring moth-eaten souls,
        crippled knees, lungs confettied by cigarettes,
and stand, quavering voices bearing rock-smooth words aloft.
        Their endurance mocks our modern habit
of making each decade a character, as if the same blood,

the same frustrations did not power all our technologies.
        But because this is today, this recording history,
I know the guitar player will die in a dozen years, so aged
        by pills and half-pints of Old Crow
his kin will have to look twice to know him.

The banjo player was probably dreaming of long-shanked women
        in red dresses as he drew the architecture
of songs about salvation and eternal light. I know
        music has always appealed to both
what is pure and what is most base in us,

cleaving us both to hopes of heaven and the dirty boogie.
        It's been years since I entered a church
for more than a polite appearance at a wedding
        or funeral, and I cannot claim
some desire to be washed in belief moved me

to lay down money for this disc of bluegrass hymns,
        remastered for a new generation.
I admit there is comfort in the smooth flow of those voices
        down the bed of familiar words,
but it is comfort I cannot wear for long.

If I could lean on that chorus, kneel
        on the banks of that river, I might know
that ancient balm, but I struck long ago
        on this dry, rocky path where
the less-tamed animals of another music wait,

soft growls gathering in their throats.

Outlasting Elegy

I'm looking out the window for the promised
meteor shower, rain of fire the heavens release,
while my thumb walks a dry pattern
on the brasswound top strings of the guitar;
wood's vibration against the bone
above my heart reminds me man's first instrument
was probably the drum. This room, hollow
as a gourd, trembles with the small beat
of my foot on the floor. If
this was a different night, if I could see
those grains of burning stone, I might
give each one the name of someone departed.
But the cold sky stays bare, the dead
fade into the carved letters of their names.
And if I stand here long enough, I'll begin
to lament deaths that have not happened yet.
There is no end to elegies. And they are all
the same elegy: Milton keening for lost Lycidias,
Shelley fighting his tears for Adonais, the blind reverend
Gary Davis singing "Death Don't Have No Mercy,"
a song I can't find in the slur my fingers rake
from these strings. When Gary Davis played guitar,
one thumb held a heart-steady rhythm
while his fingers danced out notes bright and uncatchable
as stars, the way that other blind singer, Milton,
crafted lush Edens with his tongue, versions of paradise
that stay although the tongue that brandished them
has gone to soil. Years after Gary Davis's death,
I can listen to him sing of salvation and lust.
I can hope for meteors. I can hope
we go on forever, like music or fire,
outlasting even the grim tolling
of elegy and our own burning skin.

Townes Van Zandt (1944-1997)

> *"all born to grow and grown to die"*
> "Rex's Blues"

It seems fitting to have forgotten
the first time I heard his voice
since so many of his songs resurrected
the swamp-dark of pre-language

we've built civilizations to deny.
He spoke of writing "Mr. Mudd and Mr. Gold"
in such frenzy it seemed his hand might fall off.
Other times he imagined having

no hands at all might cure the soul-deep
terror that carved long caverns through him.
Our oldest music lies buried
in such night-blankness, bone rattling bone,

clawed fingers drumming stretched hide,
sound whose ferment helps us forget
our short wait for death. The first time
I saw him play, a man spoke from the front row,

saying they'd lived on the same street as boys,
biography we didn't expect of someone
so thoroughly built of wind and ash,
his face a collage of hollow bone and slant rhyme.

"Is that you, Bill?" Townes did not quite smile
as he squinted down a valley mapped
with broken strings, uncapped pints, nightmares
written on envelopes. He shook hands, then,

delicate as a spider dances, finger-picked "Colorado Girl."
If you hear his thirty years of records, time pulled

his voice deeper and slower, distilled it
with regret, with vodka and cigarettes and sleep

that brings awake a thirst that is fire
joining fire. And the songs change.
A rambunctious boast—"Guess I'll keep a rambling/
Lots of booze and lots of gambling"—becomes

clear-eyed self-elegy for a man
who would bet on whether
the numbers on the gas pump ended up
odd or even. "Daddy's having a fight

with his heart," was how his daughter reported
the last struggle of his life. Six months before that,
I watched him, shaky with living and booze,
which was, by then, the same thing,

as he hacked at his guitar, losing his way
through words many of us knew like breathing.
No one spoke or stopped watching. Finally, silently,
he stepped into the off-stage dark, giving

the club to the cave-deep quiet
you can hear on some of his last recordings
when the stretch for a note or a word
echoes the fight to control

the first instrument, the struggling heart.

"Where Late the Sweet Birds"

in memoriam, Tommy Flanagan

Birds loop and spin outside the stone gates
        of winter's fortress, descending
only to pick stubborn ground, never completely
        disappearing from this place where winter
is mostly improvised and the week that finds
        bird tracks scrawled in snow is followed
by the week of muddy thaw.
                In here,
    Sunset and the Mockingbird, the concert
recorded on your sixty-seventh birthday changes
        the season cast over our downstairs rooms,
and as much as I might wish to claim
        some forewarning of your now-arrived absence
from those tunes, each song refuses
        to give up the bone-rattling life
your attention granted them.

* * * * *

        So who will sing for you, old elegy-maker?
Who will play for you as you played
        for Ella, Monk, Coltrane, Thad Jones,
spirits already flown,
                spirits
I might once have claimed waited to add
        your harmony to their passing names,
but it seems clear now that we are
        brief passages, bound only by the framing
artifice of music, of speech and geography,
        the invented ways of tying
one life to another,
                of denying
the silence each note falls to.

* * * * *

     We have descended to the short days,
their light a spark grudged from flint,
    the air a cousin to stone,
                         when the gathering chill
demands from us the deliberation
     I saw from you at Memorial Hall
the single time I saw you play, your dry patter
    between songs leaving us unsure
whether to laugh or not. And somewhere
     in the second set, as the bass player bent
further into his already too-long solo,
    you shared a shrug and quick grin
with Kenny Burrell, the two of you waiting
    for the cascade of deep notes to end
so you could get to work.

* * * * *

     On the job sites and in the warehouses,
a radio was always hammering
    against the bicker over which station
to play.
     A hand was always reaching
to take the music from soul
    to heavy metal and back.
                       The Detroit car factories
were no place for music but the workers brought
    their swollen hands and tired backs, their ears,
pounded nearly deaf by steel on steel
                    to leave behind their jobs
while you did yours,
     nodding in time to the quiet craft
learned during a thousand nights
    at the long-flown Bluebird that taught you
to follow melody down the most-tangled path.

* * * * *

This is weather we earn
        our passage through, when even the warmest music
becomes a fist of seeds scattered
        across dry and stony ground. This is not
elegy, only one more map of a season
        when you became a flurry of notes waiting
to rise from wiser hands than mine,
        to shade the horizon long enough
to gather our attention and briefly enough
        to be named beautiful
even though such quick disappearing wants
        the body's song to fly with it.

Ballads

The first lesson slow songs teach
is that the strength most needed
by musicians does not live
in hands spidered by sinew
but in hearts able to time
how breath rises to sweet fog.
Making it sound easy is
a trick the real players find.
The first cry through the gut-curve
of a horn might yield nothing
but tuneless groans that rattle
air and metal. Later come
the long disciplines of breath
that carry notes into dreams,
let them shine between sleep and thought.
And if radio's small voice
lets a blue slur of trumpet
lace the small hours of night
before falling to silence
that can outlast all music,
you can believe you were there
to hear the first breath flower
into song, lighting the road
music has always been, not
the one pursued to lay claim
to some prize but to sing joy
in a body driving home
through night's unsearched hours,
free to take the unknown road
that leans back before the touch
of headlights and bends the way
soft music gives way to air,
making us bend close to hear
the chorus we know will come
before the band takes it home

because there is no end in sight
and all night, still, to get there.

Toolshed

Given enough space, each man believes
he could raise cathedrals, construct
furniture whose nails would outlive
six generations, so he stakes
claim to some part of the basement,
a corner of the garage, even
a small building divided from
the hothouse of family noise
where most of his life is rooted.
There, he might stand amid
drafty fumes of gasoline, sawed wood,
and the smell that, thick as old dust,
bakes deep in the handles of tools,
combustion of sweat, sore fingers,
old solvents. Bunker of small labors,
this is where husbands repair
for the quiet beer, the unfettered cigarette
while sorting nut, bolt, washer
by size into baby food jars.
The larger tasks—lamp
that demands rewiring, table leaning
on the absence of a leg—lie
incomplete, monuments
to the ambition of self-reliance.
See how the ordered tools hang,
box wrenches and saw blades arranged
largest to smallest, orange cords
coiled tight. Brother of labor,
what comes here needing repair
is often fixed without lifting a single tool.

The Abandoned Farm

Whoever lived here last, whatever they hoped to raise, they must have
        seen more
                in those first hopeful days
than long weeds covering any trace of the way to the house

            that leans, disappointed,
gutted now, and weakened by years of weather, into
                the unmowed growth

of a yard that has become a field, that waits now to be claimed
                by a developer's earth mover
or by kudzu that already loops and binds the trees, a graying barn.

            Because I love what is fallen
or falling, I stopped on the road's shoulder to follow
                the wink of light

from the single window tucked under the eaves, the only one
                unbroken, and pushed my way
toward the peeling roof whose top peak still peers

            above this green tangle.
More warning than enticement, it calls me anyway, dares me
                to guess at what is not

told by the little left here. Back-to-the-landers I bet myself,
                renting this sharecropper house
to try and coax food enough from their lost field, to make their own

            ashy soap and candles,
chop their own wood, to grow the wilderness they dreamed
                during lectures

on Emerson and Brook Farm, lectures that managed not to mention
        the bark of callous
that grows on hands, the furrow of pain the back becomes beneath the weight

        of constant maintenance
such life requires. I used to see those couples at the farmer's market or food co-op,
        truck more battered each season

clothes a collage of patchwork, their children knot-haired and feral,
        begging for candy and sodas,
while their parents thumbed produce or weighed flour and corn meal,

        calculating to
the last biscuit what they needed against what they could afford.
        Some hung on to learn

what was useful, orthodontically straightened teeth browning a bit
        as their voices forgot
the classroom murmur, as their gardens greened

        and their candles stopped
sputtering and whispered hours-long light. Others, like the ones who lived here
        slipped away, leaving

only the woodstove that is still here, rusted to the same orange
        as the clay staining my shoes;
they wake now with hands made soft by giving thanks

        for toilets that flush,
cars that start each morning, for fire merely decorative,
        not the single means of cooking

and heat. When a finger begins to trace the iron scrollwork on the stove,
        the story comes clear
because there is no beginning here and no ending, only

                    a starting place
and a spot where the finger lifts from a track endless
                    as the work of raising

a life out of mud. This house will serve as no monument; soon
                    even its mute testimony
will be done and its slow abandonment will become one more

                    verse in the story
of the struggle that belongs to all of us who have
                    hands and breath, who have

lives able to stand and sometimes even to flower
                    against weeds that come
to choke and cover it, against blades that reach to cut it flat.

The Vermeer Moment

Say it is a gathering, a slow
coming on that whispers
this world might be made
not of noise and distraction only,
but a mosaic of pauses,
tiny limbos: the cork plied
from the mouth of the bottle,
the wooden match just scratched
into fire, the instant of air
and wine tending one another
before the golden weight
in the bottom of the glass
the hand raises into the ribbons
of sun lacing through curtains
to darken the wine to the shade
of honey, nearly amber, color
the tongue aches to hold.
In such stillness we believe
we can read the question
hanging between the offer
and acceptance of a gift
or in the gaze of a picture's
one tenant who watches someplace
beyond the picture's plane
of vision. This is
how we recall one another,
not by motion but gesture:
head bent to an angle,
the rib of light that scores
your knife as you chop
peppers to warm our soup,
because, once, a handful
of times, the patient confluence
of brush and paint and light held
those figures long enough

to let us see through them
to the moment of paint's flowing
into motion, into the next word
being said, the hand making
the incomplete gesture, the visitor,
long-awaited, now visible
on the crest of an unseen hill.

Narrative and Dirge

First morsel of spring and the old fit of shoveling has me again.
                It's a flower bed I'm turning dirt for
this time, a needed fringe of color along the house's bare back wall,

        but the first task is
to excavate the strata of gravel and glass, the old cigarette packs
                and rust-thickened nails

buried through the eight decades of building and rebuilding
                that mark this place
since the first carpenter tugged the first string tight

        to mark the front wall
of the house just before the metal tooth of a pick first rose
                and broke the dirt. This morning's news

was of a mine explosion, of petulant earth rearing into fire
                as pockets of trapped gas
discharged, throwing the men working the mine like toys

        to be lost or broken
in the tantrum of earth's crust. Such grave news would once
                have become a ballad

frailed by thin voices and archaic strings, stanzas
                dark and hard-edged
as the coal those suddenly missing men battered from dirt and rock,

        not fodder
for a wind-chiseled reporter posed before the flare
                of emergency lights, before

the slag pile that rises near the mine's entrance to drink
                all light from the sky.
"Jesus Saves" read the dripping blue letters on a sign

              I pass each morning, a sign
fashioned from boards torn from the side of one of the tarpaper-sided
   tobacco barns
                  built to replace

the old mud and log barns, that were themselves replaced
                      by the silvery tin barns
whose shine grows more cloudy each year, the rust

                that loosens their seams
mute agreement that they will be replaced one day by houses
                    built in neat rows, each made

according to one of three floorplans, bright linoleum and hardwood
                        covering acres that once were dust
and seed. I worked one summer for an archaeologist, opening pits

                in a field he'd paid
a farmer not to plant. And I stayed with that excavation
                  long enough to uncover

a human skeleton, still mostly intact, where it had lain
                  for eight centuries
just below the shallow and tangled roots of the peanuts

                that usually loaned
the field its profit. That summer I learned a new way
                to use the shovel,

scraping the flat blade with a file until it shed a needle's gleam
                  and I could shave up dirt
by centimeters instead of the full-hearted armloads

                I'm throwing now. A few feet
from the skeleton, I uncovered an arrowhead hewed
                from white quartz

and, against all scientific protocol, raised it for a moment
                that might have been song
before I began shaping the dirt pedestal where it would sit,

        holding its buried depth
while our attempts at resurrection cut more deeply into dirt.
              Perhaps Jesus saves,

but he may arrive too late for the believer who,
              half-buried in coal and rock,
breathes from a pocket of air already folding around him.

              For years he surrendered his body
to the cramped veins drilled through earth's shoulders and emerged
                  into night-black,

so mineral-worn that no scrubbing could free his flesh
              to the gentle pink of birth
or soften the hands that soiled fresh towels on his way

              to touch again
the endless wealth of his wife's skin, to marvel once more that after
              extracting tons of coal from earth

he can still read the small breaks and pressures, the unhealed faults
              beneath her calm skin.
For two days my first wife and I sat by our TV watching efforts to rescue

              a two year old buried
in a dry well, listened to reporters mine that mishap
              the way scholars once mined

the coal-rich hills for songs. The girl was saved,
              not by prayer or forgiveness,
but by shovelwork that makes the body a machine

                      but a machine capable
of grace. Our marriage, already collapsed and weary of explosions,
                  caved a few months later.

Emergency crews will labor hours or days to reach the miners,
              will move fallen tons
of the same earth that will, in months or weeks, part grain by grain

                for tentative blades
that push their way into the narrative and dirge of this world
              where the dirt,

the broken pebbles of pottery scraped from a field, the praying
            or unpraying dead
all become artifact, all become one part of our singing.

The Final Part of Dreaming

Because my sleep is confusion and amnesia,
I never quite believe others' clear recollections
of what transpires behind their closed eyes.
Each morning on my drive to work,
I pass a field of thick-haunched cattle,
their heavy eyes and flapping tails betraying
no hint of ambition, no acknowledgment
of any world beyond the next green mouthful.
Some mornings a covey of birds rises,
one-minded, from the wiry grass
or swoops from the power line, smoke-shaped cloud
crossing the wide screen of my windshield,
the inspiration for such moments as unsayable
as the shapes haunting the alleys of our sleep.
I've seen the legs of my sleeping dogs shiver
and twitch, heard them whimper
at what pursued them. My wife wakes
murmuring a collage of image and memory
or tells me of some misdeed I committed
in the funhouse of her sleep, mock betrayal
followed by mock forgiveness. If they aren't
spoken out loud, they vanish, she says,
quick birds crossing the horizon.
My recollections of dreams retreat from language.
If I tried retrieving them, they would only be
the jagged shapes of prehistoric birds,
shadows darkening the margins of sky.
The tongue is the body part most like a wing,
its directions as unpredictable as they are sudden.
My friend who went on a ten-day retreat
of silent meditation said the quiet grew
so thick in his ears that one morning
he woke to hear himself talking, words flying
from the black nest of his mouth.
He did not recognize his own voice.

The nightly soaring from the body needs
no explanations; it perches instead, vulture-silent,
on the broken branch of the tongue,
the last place dreams find to rest.

Toast

While the coffee maker surges, light
inserts itself between object and object

until I can say *dogwood*, say *car*,
say pattern cut from night's fading quilt.

By the time the pot fills, our windows stare,
blank with day's pre-sun white.

This will be day's last moment
still enough to grasp what is gone, what is missing.

The night before my father's funeral, I sat up
with my brother, pouring bourbon over new wounds

until sun bled through black trees;
birds that knew to keep hidden called,

and we had to stand and walk through a day
we had saved ourselves from imagining

because this day would give shape
to all the days without mercy

coming at us, series of shadeless moons,
nights hot and restless as pitch,

each hour secret from the next.
I pour my cup full, let the scald

bite my tongue. I see now we had the wrong drink:
coffee's the toast to grief,

something dark and bitter that will not let you sleep.

Testimony

How silly the years of meetings, of working steps
        to measure an endless journey's progress,
                the cups of bad coffee,
offer no better argument against drinking
        than the platitudes that pursed his mouth

the first time he heard them. The voice on the phone
        is holding a half-gallon of cheap vodka
                the way some suicides hold
the gun or blade they plan to use, waiting
        for the weapon to surrender its menace.

If he was asked, he would say he never wanted
        to write down his phone number for the shaking man,
                but his sponsor told him
to give his help to anyone who asked.
        So he did. Now the voice wobbles between

threats and begging, and he tastes again
        the acid splash of rage coughed up in his throat
                the night his wife tried
to pull a drink from his fist, how he pulled away
        so hard it was nearly a blow, his arm curling

to strike as the drink spilled. Then they were silent,
        their breath deep and helpless. She was gone by morning.
                His father used to come home
singing songs from the radio, the words all wrong
        as he made a sloppy drink. No words are

the right ones to quiet the carping voice or the fear
        that comes with being needed. He called no one
                on his sleepless, shaking nights,
frightened that any flinch marked him for failure.
        Sometimes he went to bed in daylight and lay

sleepless until the next morning. He must have learned
           something in those hours besides sentences recycled
                     from the Big Book or slogans
hung in the room where he goes twice a week,
           coffee going cold as he listens

for words he does not hear although he hopes
           they will be said each night. When the voice says
                     tell me why I shouldn't drink,
he speaks to kill the silence he kissed
           to life when the glass was against his lips.

Translating the Dogwood

Who can negotiate the shadow-web
cast by the calm dogwood
that did not blaze but whispered
its way into full blossom?
Soon I'll walk outside to drink in
how gently the season has turned,
sneaking in like the guilty husband who,
shoes in hand, eases open the back door,
tip-toes up the creaking stairs. Yet,
each year one more of the dogwood's limbs
dies into bone, no longer dreaming
the green fire of new buds. In the story
my friend told of her mother's moving
out on her father, each day they carried
one or two pieces of furniture away,
arranging what remained
around each new absence until
the emptiness was too great to deny.
But by then they were gone. It was spring
and although they were broke,
her mother planted flowers until
their yard was a banked fire
of color. The world tells stories
we should do our level best to listen to,
but the slow-growing riot outside lets me
believe that whatever this earth has
to tell is written best in the calligraphy
of shadow the twice-damned dogwood lets
fall over soft grass, in the lisp of wind
humming under new leaves, in this dirt
we stand rooted in, no matter
how we aspire to blossom or flame.

The Burning Between Fires

> *"It was meant to be beautiful, the hosts striving*
> *for that, but not meant to be*
> *as beautiful as it was."*
>
> Suzanne Cleary

If our afternoon of holiday shopping
had not lagged into night,
we would not have seen the graveyard
glowing in the dark that falls

hard and early this time of year.
At the head of each grave a luminary glowed,
lung of candle-flame turning
the white paper bag that housed it translucent,

the way breath burns the body into motion.
We entered between stone pillars to steer
our silent way among tiny fires.
From the road, each single flame was lost in the haze

of light hovering knee-high above the graves,
but when we drove among them or paused
to spy down a single row, we could see
how some flames surged while others wavered

the way some lives devour all that lies before them
while some limp along, never quite taking hold.
At the back of the graveyard, we stopped
to take in the eye-filling symmetry.

Whatever combination of faith and time worked
to create in that cemetery a shine that muted
the sky's pepper of stars, they must have visioned
a neat whole choiring welcome or farewell,

not each flame laboring in solitude,
heat and thoughtless motion unwinding
from its blue core to dissolve the candle's body
to hard puddles of wax that pooled

on the sand that rooted each candle stalk.
However that field was intended,
it cast a beauty we saw through
to what burned between each fire.

Even at its center, it seemed illusion,
and now, twisted in memory's scratched lens,
describing it reminds me of nothing
so much as a trick a friend performed at parties:

setting fire to lighter fluid cupped in his palm.
Done correctly, the flame vanished before
the flesh felt more than slight warmth,
and the eye registered only a quick blossoming

of flame burning the hand empty
even as we leaned forward
to be sure of what we had seen
and wanting to see it again.

The Song In the Background

A moment comes in the movie *Magnolia*
when the camera drifts between the film's
several unhappy characters to find each
singing or mouthing the words of the song
in the background, while the apocalyptic
rain of movies falls, filling the legendary
concrete riverbeds of Los Angeles.
The rivers I know best are bedded
in mud, run undammed and slow,
their hidden muscles of current lounging,
hazardous as grief, below the brown skin of water
that, like grief, looks easier to cross
than it is. If you can believe
so many off-key singers, so many fates
joined by a single chorus, then you can
believe the frogs that suddenly fall
at the movie's end, out of
the up-to-now indifferent sky,
balls of blood and air bursting fierce and Biblical
on a land that dreamed its existence
scripted for escape from judgment and prophecy.
We escape nothing. Tonight I have tried
to write a letter to the wife
of my dead teacher and friend, but my words run
slick as the well-mapped passage of water
along spillways of concrete more accustomed
to wine drinkers and skateboarders than sudden gravities
of water whose one aim is to join
other water. When rain drives the surfaces
of brown rivers to a boil, they run
light and reckless for a few days, beckon
finger-thin canoes to wing the seething
alleyways of trees, past foundations
of fallen and abandoned mills,
into the sudden green flatness of fields

whose distances of radio towers and tin-roofed barns
summon the judgment no land escapes.

Hour of Possibility

The downtown buildings that loom
over the treeline catch
the sun's descent in their glass-paned fronts
so thousands of reflected suns
burn into a single sheet
of fire, slur of gold that turns
the center of this city
to a burnished valley. Watching
from my front porch, I'm tempted
to believe the luminist painters
or the sunsets conjured
on Hollywood soundstages,
all that end-of-the-world fire
and music a promise
of what endures. Even broken things
soften in this hour
of possibility, hour between
labor and nightfall, when
sins are easy to dismiss
and desire seems endless
as the sight of her shoulders
flushed a slow and deepening
red against our sky-blue sheets
this morning before the slow
commerce of the day began.
However many more days there are
of this, I want every one,
and from each one I want
the small beauty that lifts us,
shining, up from ourselves,
into moments we would not trade
for any part of earth, not while
the eternal stands so close.

Al Maginnes has appeared in numerous publications, including *The Georgia Review*, *Quarterly West*, *Bellingham Review*, *Crab Orchard Review*, *Mid-American Review*, *New England Review*, and others. He has published two volumes of poetry, *Taking Up Our Daily Tools* (St. Andrews College Press, 1997), which won the Oscar Arnold Young Award from the North Carolina Poetry Council, and *The Light in Our Houses* (Pleaides Press, 2000), which won the Lena Miles Wever Todd Competition. He teaches at Wake Technical Community College in Raleigh, NC.

DATE DUE			
NOV 28 2011			
OCT 02 2015			
GAYLORD			PRINTED IN U.S.A.

JAN '06